BEWILDERED BY ALL THIS BROKEN SKY

BEWILDERED BY ALL THIS BROKEN SKY

Poems by Anna Scotti

LIGHTSCATTER
PRESS

Printed in the United States of America

Cover art: Yellow-billed Cuckoo from Birds of America (1827) by John James Audubon, etched by William Home Lizars. Original from University of Pittsburgh. Digitally enhanced by rawpixel. Public Domain CC0 Image ID: 277175.

Cover design: Kayden B. Groves

Author photo credit: Victoria Scotti

Lightscatter Press is an independent nonprofit literary press with 501(c)(3) tax-exempt status, that seeks to preserve and extend the material, tactile experience of the printed, bound text through beautiful, innovative design that integrates digital artifacts and experiences created for and with the printed text. Our home is Salt Lake City, Utah.

Library of Congress Control Number: 2021931889
Names: Scotti, Anna, author
Title: Bewildered by All This Broken Sky, Poems by Anna Scotti
Description: Salt Lake City, Lightscatter Press (2021)
Identifiers: Library of Congress Control Number 2021931889 | ISBN 9781736483503 (trade paperback)
LC record available at *https://lccn.loc.gov/2021931889*

First Printing

Lightscatter Press
Salt Lake City, UT
www.lightscatterpress.org

We're Always About to Begin

The Soul of the Bear

What We Wished For

That Thing You Did

It's All Shadows and Cats

'A passage through varied ambiences'

A dérive is an idea described by Guy Debord as a 'technique of rapid passage through varied ambiences,' wherein one lets oneself be 'drawn by the attractions of the terrain and the encounters' one finds there. (From The Bureau of Public Secrets. *https://bit.ly/3pjigEn.*) When you encounter a QR code on the pages of this book, scan it with your camera phone—this will take you to an alternate path through *Bewildered by All This Broken Sky*.

[https://www.lightscatterpress.org/bewildered-by-all-this-broken-sky/digiital-derive]

For Victoria,
of course

We're Always About to Begin

Now That I Have Known Loss

So many summers ago that I doubt you are alive to recognize yourself, the old Galahad of my poem—but let's start with the baby, pushing her own stroller with fat starfish hands, while you, sullen neighbor of drawn drapes and noise complaints, carried a bag of trash as tidy and neatly knotted as yourself, frowning as if even a sour nod might cost you, as if the sun weren't beating glitter from the sidewalk, scattering diamonds in our path. How odd, to find myself the villain, and never know until this moment. I'll admit I was a barefoot slattern of a mother; I'll admit I should have kept that fat hand tucked tight within my own. She knocked the stroller down our steep drive and you leapt, slipped, and rose in bloody triumph, stroller clutched in a gnarled fist, to find the child safe against my knee. How odd, to realize now that old men are just men, as foolish with chivalry as any callow nineteen. Now that I have known loss, I know what you wished to spare us. Now that my bones ache, I know what that leap cost you, and the reckoning: my daughter's bright sharp laugh, my pretty hand extended as you sprawled, cursing, casting shadows in the drive.

Tanager

There are people who spend this pink hour of dawn walking the perimeters of skyscrapers in Houston, never looking up, gathering birds that have crashed against the great walls of mirrored windows, bewildered by all this broken sky and endless squares of cloud. And there is a Texas man who crosses to Matamoros every morning, stacks of flyers on the cracked seat beside him: *La has visto? Missing seven years.* They are never coming back, the girl, the years, they are never coming back, the flocks that once darkened the plain wide skies like purple clouds, but there are goldfinch, and warblers, and martins tucked in every tree, nature's secret, until their desperate hallelujah at the orange edge of dawn. Some of the birds are dead and some will die on folded towels in boxes tucked beneath desks or in car trunks, old women's tears wetting the broken beaks, the perfect feathers, but a few will be released to wing again into the treacherous sky. Now the wayward daughter dances for a slab-faced man whose fists bristle with folded dollars, or she washes laundry for beans and oranges, or she has lain at the bottom of a rocky ravine since the morning of the slammed door, since her father's words were spoken; that can't be undone. But here a scarlet-throated bird is cupped in a man's rough palm, a thick finger strokes its bright breast, and in response, a trembling.

Fairgrounds

Turning back, you find
that the fat orange candy-coated moon
is just that, a moon. The wheel that spun and dropped
and rocked—where you threw your head back
and screamed dares at an electrified sky—
is just a wheel, metal and paint, gears ground smooth,
no longer trusted not to slip and lose their way
on what ought to be a simple trip—around
and around. Stopped wheel. Cold moon.
And where the carnival was, asphalt and spilled soda,
wind-whipped flyers advertising something new and shiny
as a copper coin, a summer sparkler, a bright brass ring.

Wishbone

Aw, to hell with world peace, curing cancer, and the polar bears.
Me, I'd grow old with my grandparents, three pairs of knobby knees
tucked up in beige rocker recliners as we pass the tea pitcher,
trading miseries—her hips, his back, my heart—but damn, we
wouldn't be young again for anything. Instead of two clasped hands,
three. Three sets of scuffed slippers, three thirds of a folded newspaper.
And if it got dull, ever, though I doubt it could, we'd open
the cracked album and remember hand-cranking peach ice cream,
picnics with the cousins after church, wading the cool waters
at the lake cabin, driving up, up, into the Blue Ridge Mountains,
all the world spread out beneath us, backseat stuffed with books
and sweaters and cold fried chicken, two wrinkled-apricot people
and their very good friend, a very old, very young, plump-thighed,
jam-mouthed, tangled-haired little girl, the kind that can't do anything
wrong, the fearless kind, greedy and fat with wishes granted,
the kind that makes even getting old look not so scary, just three
good buddies on the big bench seat of a '66 Olds Cutlass Supreme,
wending our way along Skyline Drive and into the purpling
cloudbanks, unafraid.

Water and Stone

Who knows if there even is a right way to do things?
Maybe I was wrong. Oh, I'm guileless, palms wide,
careful to ease the time-fold between my eyes;
it bears witness that I'm angry, when I'm not.

I'm not. And here on the bright grass, air stirring
all around, a bird's cry and silvery balloons there, weighted
by a stone, you'd think we could talk for once, that he'd crack
that dry silence, tell me, *Don't worry, then, we all*
make mistakes. Or he could simply touch my hand, trace
the lifelines on the palm, or let his lashes move against
my skin and I would know. I'm listening. But it's a silence
that won't be broken; not like rock after all, but fluid, filling
every crack and finding its own level, its surface as perfect and
shining as the brown skin of the pond. A man is watching from
the shadow, jangling keys: the gates must close,
the bird has flown, the scent of ripening flowers is heavy
on the darkening grass.

They never speak, the guard would like to tell me. *Their silence*
is what holds against the steady push of stone. But his shift
is ending and his poor feet ache, or his wife's on graveyard,
or the baby's sick, and I am kneeling on the grass, calling out
in a language never spoken anymore.

Jellyfish

Yesterday, reading finally by day what I'd long known
by night, working Bruegel faces from the cratered stucco
of the ceiling, pushing back the dreadful thing, the known
and not known, yesterday I pressed my palm flat
against your pixelated face and whispered, *gone.*
Not Fallujah or Baghdad or Kentucky, this time, but
really, *gone.* And I thought of your young wife, her grief,
her small fists, that smart cap she brought from Ukraine,
so blue and rich against her smoky hair, and I thought
of your fatherless child. You're a bedtime story now,
old friend. A promise left unkept, a bordered box
on a folded page. And I remembered snorkeling a blue
cave off Maui, coaxing my new husband, so afraid
of the invisible life that swarmed and snapped against
our fresh skins. *Jellyfish,* the captain claimed, and at last
my husband dropped my hand and slipped beneath
the sparkling surface, already kicking away.

Then Fall Again

Orange, gold, crunch, crisp. Apples cut in clean crescents, burnt marshmallow, smoke caught in the folds of our jackets, in our hair. Luminaria pumpkins like ambassadors of the season, a mustache drawn with scorched cork, then a pilgrim's hat of black and white. Cranberries bright as blood, a cold drift from beneath the door. Crackle of ice. Spring, finally: silly to think all this could end, when everything is bursting! Buds furled tight along the branch, wet and new, a girl's soft hair, hard-soled shoes, rain against the pane and the smell of cut grass, loam and soil and sod, blossoms on the sidewalk, petals on our shoulders and days to spend, days to waste, hours sifted through our fingers like spilled sugar from the bowl. Then summer's small fruits, hard and sour, hot sidewalk, hot forehead, hot breath of August at the window and still no way to warm you, huddled at the heater, stifling wool and cups of tea and soup and steam, stained sweater, stinking socks, tissues knotted on the floor and all the ways we meant to say goodbye forgotten, no ferry now to Coronado, no starlit swim at Mazatlan. Nothing matters but to make you warm. Then fall again: orange, gold, crunch, crisp, bones and stones and broken brown leaves. One without you, then all the rest the same.

Heaven

Is heaven the dust-ridged pillow
where I kept my white leather diary,
or my sisters stalking and hissing like jealous cats,
or my father's uncleared throat: *will you pipe down, damn it—*
that could be heaven, or the dappled spaniel curled
on a sprung cushion on our cold kitchen floor.
Now the smaller sister's eyes fill, her dainty fingers curling
into a glistening white snail, a fish,
something both living and insensate.
The older sister flips her hair back, then, and I stand,
caught in a loose fold in the fabric of time,
smelling the cut lemon she tapped behind her ears
and knees the summer the canary died,
the summer I was fifteen, and feckless, in cork platforms
and chipped nails, and that straw cowgirl hat that tied
beneath the chin. That could be heaven.

And so, no longer bound by bickering, by tears,
my mother's rising laughter,
as the years fall away like dresses tried once,
and left in silken heaps all along the path
to the silvered bathroom glass, I will stand, bound
only by their beauty, my father's shout, the homey
smell of dog and the grip of my own flesh, wrapped tight
around my bones again. *Oh, beautiful girl,* I whisper.
Oh, beautiful, beautiful girl—

Hauntings

When you're lonely for the dead
you can tempt them, sometimes
with a meal, a scarf, a scrap of paper
the lucky nickel you won
on the Santa Cruz Boardwalk
the day that Chester kissed you.

Or hum something:
the show tunes from your third grade play,
that song that Albert whistled when he walked on stilts
or worked logarithms in his head.
Choose something they remember, too,
with equal longing
enough to forgo the wings, the cobwebs,
the spooky whisperings
those tedious perquisites of the dead.
Choose wisely and
Grandma will sit up late
right there at the formica table
you hauled to the dump in 1986
slicing berries over cut pound cake while
Albert reads, at last, the cold pages of your letter
that came back marked
unknown.

Save Me a Slice of Raisin Toast, Maybe a Yellow Tulip, and a Seat Close to Yours on the Red Velvet Couch

In heaven the chemistry teacher's gangling roommate will bake pies
they'll share openly, licking the juice from each other's fingers and
tumbling like bear cubs drunk on late summer berries. That dog
you abandoned when you fled Baltimore will move shyly around
your knees as you rinse her bowl at the rusted tap, and the fat girl
you mocked in fourth grade? She's a slim pretty thing in an apricot
sheath, waiting to show you her prom pictures. Even the storekeeper
you teased, then cheated, even the exhausted salesgirl you cursed
and hung up on: all's forgiven. Remember the time you wished
your grandmother dead? She died, of course, and now she's
in heaven waiting to laugh it off and serve you a steaming
plate of baked lasagna or some homemade raisin bread.
In heaven your kids will text you the best possible news
from earth, where they are happy, and their father will still love you
the way he did that sweltering summer the youngest was conceived:
bringing cups of lemon ice and asking questions about your boss—
except in heaven, you won't have one. In heaven, you lent your brother
the money the first time he asked. You never brushed the hair
from your niece's boyfriend's eyes, and that thing at the drugstore in
1996? Never happened! So what if heaven's not real? There's a special
room for non-believers, and your seat is on the red velvet sofa, beside
that kindergarten teacher who knelt to knot your laces so tenderly.

There's the fledgling bird you kept in a shoebox, there's the clumsy
sneakers your dad bought at the discount mart; now they fit, and the vamps
are stitched with valentines. You're pretty. There's that guy
you glimpsed from a cold city bus, the one who should have chased you,
bold with longing, trailing yellow tulips. In heaven, he'll catch you
if you want him, flowers falling all around. You will hear your mother's
laughter, coming ever closer. Let's sip cool tea. No more
aching for the polar bears, cubs slipping from their bony chests—
here they slide from pristine cloudbanks to seal-rich
waters. Sweet-faced cows graze in fragrant pastures,
and in heaven every bird keeps her feathers. Don't
fret. It's heaven. Now close your eyes.
We're about to begin.
We're always
about to
begin.

The Soul of the Bear

Grief

A squat black bakelite thing, with a coiled cord
and a smug pug face, your thin fingers tangled
in the wire, and all of us watching from the table,
wishing you'd shrugged and let it ring. But no voicemail
then, no caller ID, no slim cell on the pillow,
delivering iconic messages through the night.
When the phone rang then, someone
meant to reach you. We passed a blue striped bowl of corn
and peas, my brothers reached for a single chop,
my sister turned, still smiling. The dog trotted
swiftly from the room as you pushed back your chair.

Or Maybe It's *Für Elise* Banged out on a Cheap Electric Organ with Sand and Cracker Crumbs Jammed Between the Keys

You could make a case for orange sunsets, waves lapping up against sand as yellow and crisp as spilled saltines, *Starry Night*, that huge tattered flag stretched out before a dozen neat seamstresses of various national origins at the Museum of American History in Washington. Then there's summer squash, gleaming yellow through the thickening vines, there at the bottom of the neglected garden, and Miss Dior tapped behind your knees and in the ripe crook of your elbow, *Black Orpheus*, and those black waves licking sand as dark and sweet as brown sugar, with a moon huge and white like a cold wheel of cheese slung low over the starless horizon, and don't forget fresh strawberry preserves, glistening against the diamond glass, the fragrance still caught beneath your nails and in the pockets of your apron. And a white knit jacket, size newborn to six weeks, soft as the belly of a tame rabbit, and cataracts of snow. And the sound of rain on cedar shakes when you've got a fresh cup of coffee, a ream of white paper, and all day. All day, and waves slapping shore, steady through the rain. And buttered cornbread, and buttercups, and violets. And that first crocus, pushing up through the matted leaves and dirty snow, just purple: the purpleness of it. And a girl on the beach, brown arms folded beneath her head, big sunglasses pushed up in her hair, belly flat and golden against her bright bikini, and the waves lapping up against sand soft and clumped like cookie dough, all that jazz. And jazz, come to think of it. Gil Scott Heron, Lady Day, Miles Davis blowing hard with his tight mean shoulders humped against the crowd. *Giovanni's Room*. John Donne, Dee Dee Bridgewater, black Ray-Bans, soft jeans and a crisp cotton shirt. The balcony scene of *Romeo and Juliet* read aloud at the local school. A single sandpiper dancing at the shoreline, waves lapping against a shore bright with bits of shell and tumbled glass as the sun drops low, low, spreading like butterscotch spilled carelessly across the blue glass table of the sea. You could make a case for leafhoppers, for sapphires, for the green piedmont of North Carolina, for a sleek grey trout circling in the cold shallows of the Little Pigeon River. It might be a leather handbag, creased and cracked and smelling of cash and perfume. It might be Daisy's puppies, fat and licked clean, or a wild horse, a brown dappled mustang, kicking in a red rock canyon in New Mexico, or your daughter reaching for your hand, or kicking toward you across an endless expanse of sunlit blue. It might be yellow, yellow, just things that are yellow and orange and gold, or the smell of fresh cut lemons, or that banana yellow sun dress that blew all around your bony knees the summer you turned seventeen.

Onomatopoeia

So promise is a girl in a loose summer dress
Hands folded neatly into heart-shaped fists.
Fist is a boy, clenched tight and hard
With bitten nails, scuffed and scarred.
Promise is a girl with scars at her wrists
Hands folded neatly into heart-shaped fists.
Heart is a muscle, thick and veined with blue
Blue is her dress, and her eyes, and a bruise.
Bruise is the taste of a plum or a peach
A stone at its heart, but yielding and sweet.
Stone is as hard and as smooth as a fist
Clean like a promise, like that first sweet kiss.

Grand Avenue

You could be excused
for not knowing it's summer,
here in the courthouse.

That thin draft smells of metal, yes,
and dust, forced as it is
from a sweating window box and not
swept from the currents of the blue ocean,
glimpsed briefly from the freeway
this dawn.
If you know the difference, the squeak
of a rubber doorstop doesn't really
sound like crickets, or sparrows trembling
on the branch.

The men are the same, winter or summer:
jocular and shaven, ties flapping, too loud
in this yellowed hall.
But look: two small girls on a marble bench
in shorts and sleeveless blouses,
bruises ripe as berries,
that purple and gorgeous,
dappling their spindly arms.

In the Big House

The bristled neck, the spots,
the hooves like blocks of stone—
they're not the oddest thing
about the great giraffe. A thick bloody rope
still hangs from her belly and you
look away, shamed somehow.
It's needless. You're like the glass,
the bars, the troughs of hay and clover,
the bulbs that dance through rusted mesh,
like sunlight through acacia, once,
like hard rain on savannah.

He takes a step, and two,
hesitates, and drops, already yielding.
Somewhere a lion moans.
She worries the calf to rise
and he butts the tough cushion of her haunch,
trembling, and breaks into fluid circles about her.
Small clean hooves
beat against the leafless floor
ringing out like a dozen bent spoons
smacked along the bars.

I See What We Must Become

—but where is the soul of the bear

dressed in a soiled tutu

and where is the soul of the elephant

that danced for peanuts and oranges, that wept

at the snap of the prod—yes, wept. All mothers can.

Where is the spirit of the dog that loped

behind the wagon, so willing to forgive,

and what of the souls of the girls, dazzled

by sequins and spangles and paint, who

sweated beneath the roustabouts, who dreamed

of home, of their schoolrooms and their cats,

and where the beaten horses,

the lizards pinned like brooches, and the soul

of the tiger that leapt through a ring

of fire—I see where we will go, must go,

but where is the soul of the bear?

Four p.m.

A thick-bodied fish
curves around a mottled stone
deep beneath the shapeless surface
of brown water.

A hawk dips low,
plummets, pierces the shining lake skin
and rises again, glistening scaled
claws clenched tight about water,
air, loss, desire.

Seven p.m.

Someone has left a shining heap
of trash fish on the dock; mostly silver,
some dappled brown, and those flash silver
at the gills. Each scale is a prism;
yellow leaf, crimson vein, gold-edged cloud.
One fish is flipping, eyes reddened,
slapping against the stiffening
heap beneath the helpless sun. *Trash fish*,
as though that were its name: *Purgamentum piscis*,
or *piscis non volo*. Beneath, the water
slaps the dock, nearly still, darkening.

405 North

It's a fitting memorial to quiet disaster,
this worn ribbon of asphalt that shimmers from the city
to the deserts north, a finite circle. Yes,
there's such a thing. Believe
in magic here, in substance wrought of smoke, in life,
then no life. This freeway is a made thing, a patched fabric
stretched taut between exhausted mountains, but it's alive
in ways you've never been, vibrating in time with the engines and
the cries of birds and chainsaws. Those spent hills,
dull with chaparral and painted concrete,
are marked with tattered bouquets and letters made
more carefully than lives are made,
and lost: *Manuel, Rolling 96. Monika RIP.*
Desiccated lizards, enough for a valise—
hell, a matched set—mark the miles. A single tortoise, cracked,
an orange satin high heeled shoe, somebody's lunchbox. Crows,
cats, possums, that brown dog that cringed against the barrier,
lie scattered at the roadside.
Rushing past you think of stopping, of—
what, then? You've no means to put an end to it, only tires.

What We Wished For

Philadelphia

I held hands with a stranger today, just reached across the aisle and tucked my clenched fist into his; his wedding ring pressed a mark into my bare knuckle. My right, his left, for the moment we were promised. A baby's cry rose above the querulous buzz; men fumbled for cell phones, banged their knees on the tray tables and cursed as the woman beside me whispered the Lord's Prayer and from the back, soft sobbing and one brave high-pitched laugh, quickly hushed.

The plane bucked and reared like a gut-twist horse, didn't roll over but wanted to, and we all felt it groan and strain against the wind and the air and all the nothingness out there, and when I looked past the praying woman through my window, cloud, and across the aisle through his window, green squares of farmland, another place I'll never see, and an overhead bin popped open and a woman shrieked, then, and the captain's words rolled over us like God's voice, that full of authority and doom; *brace*, and there was the stranger's hand, clutching the narrow armrest, pale and broad, thickly veined, and my eyes met his, my hand met his, and when it ended, finally, and the flight attendant pushed through the cabin, crisp and resolute, as if her makeup were not streaked with tears, as if she hadn't been just now head in hands, calling for her mother and her cat, then he made her wait and she waited patiently as he lifted my white fist to his dry lips and kissed each knuckle tenderly, set my hand back on my lap as carefully as you might set a fledgling on its branch, and turned again to his folded newspaper, and sighed.

T'es Pas Seule

Cracked windshield, hot shaft of light.
Peek-a-boo: skinny arms flung up against
the roof; so still. She might be dazed,
asleep, chapped pale lips just slightly parted—
but bricks are tumbled across
the hood like wooden blocks, like dominoes.
No fire, just smoke, and the smell
of oiled leather thick against the coiled heat.
The wreck settles and sighs, clearly exhausted.
Hush, I whisper foolishly, but she could be still
hovering, confused by all the stillness,
by the sirens coming near. The door groans
and yields and I crouch beside her, touch her cool
throat and speak in every language I can muster:
vacation French and bus stop Spanish,
English that clings to my tongue,
unwilling: *No estás sola, querida.*
Todo está bien. Tranquille, chérie.
T'es pas seule. Rest easy, rest easy,
 you aren't, just yet, alone.

The Definition of Ballistics

It could be a kind of dance
bodies twirling, jerking, *balançoire,*
as if held aloft by some invisible force—
or it's math, arcane and incomprehensible,
a strange algebra with impossible sums paid
and due and marked in red. And there the child,
soiled tutu knotted about her soft belly
as she leaps, shouts something that's not quite right
for this bright dance, and an older girl *brisé,*
jeté, and a boy, glasses knocked carelessly aside—perhaps
he tired of his numbers, and the dappling of light
that fell down on his fingers as they danced
across the ledger—tired, sprawled as he is
across the cold court, pencils scattered,
and the sirens, and the girl who leapt, and kicked,
and cried, has dropped to her knees, her hands
in his shirt and on his mouth and in his hair,
scrabbling there, and the clumsy danseuse stops,
and now, just silence.

Gaia

Girl, you disappoint. I really thought you'd fight back, but you're a mattress. A lay-down. Grouchy, yeah, we get it: hurricane, tsunami, blizzard, heat wave. Temper, temper. All your storming won't change a thing. Fracking, that's *us* giving *you* earthquakes. You've got gill nets tangled around your bottom half like soiled garters, forests of scorched trunks like ragged nails on ringless fingers. Your veil is a venomous mist, your crown a cloud of poisoned smoke. I bet you thought this generation would rattle your bones, your bridegroom come at last, you poor old mother. Nope. We are the frat boys to your virgin. The factory farmer to your sweet-uddered cow. We are the kind of kids that throw out the batter but lick the bowl clean, then break the bowl. And if we could, bitch, we'd leave you to clean up the mess.

Did You See Us This Morning, at the Station at Six?

Poised on the platform, balanced on my toes, tipped forward as if I'd never heard of the third rail, of sweating men in sweatstained shirts, of packs of teens pushing women to the tracks for sport, like keying cars, like cars afire, cats afire, the world's on fire, I rock, squeezing my fists to my ears against the sound of my own thoughts and realize, then, I've forgotten what I knew of quadratic equations, of iambic hexameter, of the periodic table, of what makes some gases noble, and what exactly is atomic mass, and I'm rocking, and my tongue no longer fits the thin flat geometrics of English, nor the gutter rolls of French, and once again I've confused free verse with blank verse when they've little in common but a disrespect for the most basic of rules. Oh, rocking there at the precipice, it's as if I've misplaced all I ever knew of danger, of pit bulls, of fire, of canyons. And I'm nearly old, and Christ, I forgot to put my face against the cascade of orange bougainvillea that tumbles over the cracked wall, though I thought of it often enough. I forgot to kneel, press my cheek to the cement, and watch brown ants hoist crumbs, larvae, impossible loads, in their frangible pincers. I forgot to lick the icicles that cling to the peeling sill. What color is the underside of a pigeon's silken wing? I scan the sparse crowd quickly, counting: younger, younger, older, younger, but now fractions escape me, and there's that thick truth in my throat, that in the end all numerators equal zero. I can think clearly, but only of the dirty man scrubbing his streaked arms outside Safeway with those bleached cloths meant to disinfect the cart handles. So full of joy, for what? Clean hands, a clean stubbled chin, strong legs that carried him away, away, and I want to go, but I don't, and I want to lie flat there, cheek to the cool rail, and know what it is to be (or not to be) and I think I've figured out at last what it is the prince is asking. So there's the question, and at least that much is clear, and there's the pounding in my heart now rising, rising, till it's my temples throbbing and I might be stroking out or maybe I'm only knowing the insistent shudder of the impending train, and then it's upon us, and a heavy woman takes my elbow in her gloved hand and tips me backward, so gently, till my heels find cement where there had been only air: cool gusts rushing at us from down the platform, and the doors hiss wide and we slip, separately, onboard the shining train.

Egg

I learned about being a mother from you,
never a mother yourself, and also not human,
but fierce and prideful in the feathered nest you made,
murderously jealous of that single perfect egg that held
nothing but promises. I remember those nights;
smoking on the patio, bitter-hearted, a miser counting
others' sins: the woman who let her toddler stand in the shopping cart,
another who moved through a parking lot with a string of them,
like brown ducklings, waddling behind, and the neat
blond Starbucks mamas with one hand on a stroller, the other slung
around a low mound of belly, gossiping into a phone
tucked beneath one ear. I recall. When I
stooped to stroke that cold egg you came at me, valiant,
beak sharp and ready, wings flapping, claws
like tiny talons, to defend.

The Passing of BeBop

Staring at my own clasped hands resting
on a polished table, one nail bitten to the scabbed
quick, another still a cerise oval, I think you asked
What more could I have done? The lawyers
have their own replies: a steady palm on your
broad shoulder, as if it might be you who needs the comforting,
a narrowing of eyes as subtle as the twitch of whisker
on a feral cat. I press my lips together into that
thin line that you mocked once, that you softened
with kissing, that you sketched on a torn menu in a smoke
choked restaurant there before the end.
I will not say, *You might have stayed*
through the passing of BeBop. You might have carried
that bright lump of feathers to the trash, or buried her beneath
the twisted avocado; you might have stroked
her breastfeathers when I was overcome with animal revulsion
as she struggled to get beneath the low water cup, without
reason or without any I could discern, beyond that feminine
instinct to hide, to be hidden, to make oneself as small as
possible before the impending dark, before the end.

The Passing of BeBop, Part Two

I might have forgotten to say
I never minded that you bit me, hard,
when I was late with the millet, or that I liked
your yellow feathers best, the frothy down
like bleached negligee beneath your silken flights.

I may have forgotten to thank you
for the time you chirped my name over and over –
you never rescued anyone from a diabetic coma or
displayed a grasp of the concept of zero, or even
assaulted a passing preacher with multilingual profanity -
but once when I cried until there was a saltwater
puddle on my cracked tile floor, you shook your bell
and called to me again and again until I lifted my head,
proving not only trans-species empathy and all that stuff,
but also that someone, even if someone
tiny and imprisoned and a thousand miles
from home, someone knew my name.

Of Course, Some Are Very Small

We spend our lives staring at clouds, wishing on stars, wondering
if there's even one god, but perhaps there are many, each existing
only when called upon with perfect faith, each perfectly formed
in the shape of our need. There's the god who believes
that atheists have souls, and a god of lost dogs, and one who
treasures desperate confidences: *dear god, make it come,*
please, dear god, don't let him get drunk tonight. There's a god
who likes you when you scream at the store clerk,
and there's one who smiles fondly when you flirt with your best
friend's teenaged son. Very little you can do or say will shock
the god of self-indulgence. There's the god who emerges like a genie,
a swirl of steam from the dryer vent, when you're home alone
and you hear the creak of a floorboard upstairs. He'll protect you,
at least until the doorknob turns. There's the horn-rimmed god
of unfinished term papers, the minor deities of fifth grade best friends
and lost bus passes and new boots and spilled change.
There are big heavy gods, bearded white men in bespoke suits
gathered at a rosewood table, and they will listen carefully when
you're bleeding, when you're lonely to the point of driving to the bridge,
when you're in a foreign jail, when your child is balding and dull
with chemo. They call themselves *the big guns* and they don't like to vote
against you; they want you to know that at least you've been heard.
There's a god who nods when you whisper, *I only want to see him again,*
or *sweet Jesus protect her,* and there's a tiny goddess, a child, really—you
could tuck her in your pocket—she's there when you curl into the pillow,
late at night, and weep.

Menagerie

For a year, I've dreamed
of hobbled horses, dolphins washed ashore,
a moaning dog with a crushed hind paw:
pathetic beasts dredged up
from my subconscious, like suffering fish
dumped on the deck of a boat
sinking too slowly to be of much good
to anyone. Oh, spare me
that night spent leading a broken mare about
the cracked sidewalks of Echo Park, the
sweatsick hours turning heavily
on our old plaid sofa, reliving the evening
our daughter learned to ice skate, or
at least to fall down, get up,
fall down.

Babba Ya

Babba-ya:
that first word that meant
everything: *milk, sweet, warm, sing,* and
I need you, need you
desperately.

And that first pair of shoes, hardly larger
than marshmallows, with soles
as soft and blameless as the skins of moles
or better, two white mice.

Babba-ya:
you, flouncing through the front hall
in loose high heels, drugstore lipstick
smeared across a mouth still bright with
braces, sweet with milk.

The Way of You

Four girls danced in rubber boots
welcoming a sunburst between thundershowers,
hand-me-down slickers discarded
as if purple clouds weren't already gathering
like bruises against the yellow sky.
Earthworms, forced from bloated soil
to sizzling brick, curled in desperate
shapes, ugly in their helplessness:
muscular strips of suffering, no
more than that.

The air was thick with ozone
and with heat, cut by the shrieks of the dainty
one, merciless in her disgust. The tomboy
stomped her brother's scarred boots, claiming
It's Nature's Way. They're only food for birds
and ants, now—as the plump one's eyes widened
in admiration. But the fourth girl knelt
on scabbed knees, silent, judging neither
the shrieking nor the stomping, but busy
at her calling: gathering worms
into the leaf-lined pocket of her folded shirttail.

Feathers of Gold

Last night you came to me, barefoot,
nightgown damp and twisted with sleep,
and said you'd lost a thing with four rooms
and no doors. *That's easy,* I said. *Your heart.*
Last night you turned, pushing the dark
from your eyes with both fists—*I'm calling and
calling but only my own voice answers*—and I
smoothed the blankets around you and whispered
echoes on water, feathers of gold. Last night
you muttered, *an acorn, a chestnut,* and *many eyes,
but cannot see,* and I knew that you would cry
out, still trembling from dreams of sphinxes
and corridors, deserts, hot breath. *Hush,* I told
you. *Never. Forever. The ocean. I will.*

That Thing You Did

Partridge

There's no time to stop; it's the strict coach today—
but she's already seen him, flopping along the median,
heedless of the hen that scolds above as cars loom close
and veer away. By the time I pull over, find a scrap
of cardboard and a stick, he's lifeless, but
for that single yellow eye, round and unblinking,
but bright enough. I scoop him up, finally,
into my bare palm and he stretches those new wings,
nearly feathered enough to sustain him. The hen
pecks at my ankles, frantic, but
even as I ease him to the rough grass they push close:
crows, a beetle, a string of ants, eager
to get on with it. If he's lucky,
a fox is watching.

After swimming there's that feral rush to eat anything—
an apple, chips, a candy gleaned from beneath the seat,
then sated, she turns those limpid eyes
toward mine. *She made a nest around him,*
so soft, lined with feathers from her breast, I say.
And it's later, way past bedtime, when I stoop
to press my lips to her smooth forehead, and the lie
that has soured my mouth for hours
melts like sugar,
sweet, away.

Red Slider

At dusk, they dropped it plunk in dark water,
squatting at the edge, heels sunk deep
in fragrant muck, crushing soft shoots of lily:
three girls, jeans stiff with mud, each scalp seared pink
at the part, throats hoarse with shrieking. And the turtle,
thick head defiantly erect, thrusting from that unsettling
creased collar, flippers long-nailed, still working
against air, then water, then the cold mud
at pond bottom, now only a ring expanding
on the stippled surface, widening, flattening,
gone.

Nine

They're almost past the age of rocks,
dirt, water, sticks, as pastime,
almost past the time to help time pass instead
of holding fast to stay upright
as it rushes all around.
It's almost lost, this ability to be lost
in soil, water, leaves, and folded flower petals,
the pleasure of each other.
Look, one cries, *a waterfall!* Which child I can't say,
they're that alike, all dirt-rimmed nails
and tangled braids, faces
closing inward now, like flowers close to dusk.
And it's lovely, silly, just
muddy water splashed from a plastic jug
finding its way through cracks in brick, wetting
the dry patches, puddling in the matted leaves
at the base of a crumbling wall.

Gravel glitters in my outstretched palm, an offering
to whatever god decides
which moments they'll remember.

Twelve

So, there you are, cross-legged, patient fingers
working tangles from the silky plume of the dog's tail,
mouth set in a stern love line exactly
like my grandmother's. You've already learned that love
is mostly duty: gathering worms after every rainfall, laying
countless broken birds to rest in tissued boxes,
grim as any village preacher. You've scabbed
knees, bitten nails—yet the new teacher's
eyes can't quite meet mine. Don't let all that beauty
confuse you: there will be a boy who does not
love you, then a man. And someday, a child,
willful as a windborne spirit, slamming doors
and windows, raging like a storm at sea—raging,
but so far from you!—then curled in a sullen circle
of music, friends, secrets that exclude you.
And I'll be a photograph on the dresser,
a folded note beneath a stack of silken scarves—
maybe this note. So, listen, now, your mother is speaking:
Don't flinch in the face of all that angry beauty; breathe.
Know what it is to have love enough to squander.

Parabola

It's bloody stuff, this making and raising of children:
all that girl mess, sure, then sex, then you're on
to milk-stained silk and tears over coffee,
for no real reason. Soon enough it's skinned elbows
and loose teeth, a spill on concrete, and that first split
in the dense meat of the heart:
a valentine refused, the best friend lured away,
that seventh grade dance where nobody asked her.

The crack widens; you on one side, her on the other,
nobody but a couple of girls with dirty fingernails
and stringy hair to help if she wakes
before dawn, choking on nightmares.
And you: frantic, arms flapping, growing small
across the widening void,
then smaller still. All the stories you never got to tell
weigh you down like the yellow cotton sling
your husband eased across your tender breasts
when the whole world was small enough
to fit within that sweet curve: his arm around you both, and
the piss-sweet, milk-sour sling your only burden, shared
and thus so light you never noticed
until it fell away.

Sixteen

It was the first thing we gave you, and the last thing we agreed on, hands clasped, gazing at you
—an impossibly tiny swaddled cocoon, a striped knit cap to disguise the distressed cone of your
silken head—your name: once bulky and oversized as a hand-me-down jacket, now tight and
shiny at the elbows, however styled; with a *y* or an *ie*, or that single jaunty *i*, writ daintily in
violet ink or scrawled in black felt marker. Once there were people who changed names the way
we change sundresses for blue jeans, blouses for sweaters, shrugging in and out of identities to
suit the vicissitudes that make us whoever it is we turn out to be: first, you were *Waking Dream*,
then *Water Burbling Over Rock. Dances Barefoot at Dawn. Loves Ducks. Fat Turkey Girl. Storm
Clouds Gathering.* Then *Aster* for your irises, like starbursts of green about a sunstruck center.
*Paddles Like Dog in Water. Small Woman of Courage. Knife Tongue. Beauty in Moonlight.
Secret Heart. Glory.*

While I'm Prostrate Before a God I Don't Believe in,

I'll also thank the gawkers—I know you would have stopped; I've done the same, slowed to be sure someone is watching over a scatter of broken strangers before speeding away—and especially those who did stop, as she sat shaking in a battered borrowed CRV, unhurt but for the dread that now shadows her face like a lace mantilla: the black guy jogging alone at night, first on the scene, who rapped on the window and coaxed *come on out, now,* even though he was a black guy jogging alone at night, and she a white-faced white girl clutching her own skinny arms as if something unspeakable had been done to her, or by her, as if it were more than smashed metal and paint, as if it mattered, and the teenagers who gathered, gaping and chirping, offering water and cigarettes and clumsy comfort, and the woman who called—*dread call in the night*—using that same bright false tone those same bright terrifying words I've used myself to call another child's mother (a girl whose mouth was a tangle of broken braces and shattered teeth, and I held her blood-soaked purse so tenderly until her mother could arrive) and the tow truck driver who warned, *be happy.* And of course the man, owner of the crumpled car, the man who spoke so patiently, who seemed to know that it was just a car, who seemed to care only that this girl, this restless reckless careless girl, this girl who might have changed everything but instead changed nothing in this twisted tangled impossibly beautiful bright dark world, that this girl was safe and whole though white and sick with dread, this girl, my daughter, my child, my only child.

Bacopa

Still marking Pope with a spit-slick pencil, she asks
Who saw you picking through the trash? For I have prayed
to the god of houseplants: make me the woman
who rescues aspidistra from the bin at the mouth
of the alley, no longer she who abandons them *in extremis,*
make me the one to grasp the withered stalk and smack
the cracked pot hard. Yes, hope springs eternal.
Let me cradle the knot of pothos roots like fledglings
in my palm, coaxing them to move secretly
within the tender soil. Make me know that even
the dumb things have need, that love is service.
This plastic stick promises blossoms
like snowfall—cascades of pristine petals, a cataract
of tiny flowers, of white-mittened hands—and there, she
asks again—*You're not going to* give *that to anybody, are you*—
shuts the book, and leans against me,
a sleepy sun dropping down behind the shelter
of the mountain. I set Bacopa on the sill
to bloom again, to die again. Suppertime.

Harlequin

It's the long way 'round for you, old girl, picking
your way from rag rug to carpet on paws no longer
trusted against polished wood, pausing
to be lifted once again to my widening lap.

Back when we were both new, before the slammed
doors and slipped collars, tipped trashcans and
forays in the night, back when we were both new—
oh! you were a dainty thing, tail a silken tassel,
prancing in your piebald coat like a tiny cow,
curled on your plaid pillow with neat crossed paws.

Now, smoothing tangles from your matted
coat, counting all the ways we've forgiven
each other—the angry shouts, the puddles at the door—
I remember you cradled to my daughter's flat breast,
her father's arm around us both. I remember
your growl of warning in the night.

Around the World in Forty Years

All my life you were waiting:
a boy too old for me, of course, smoking and spitting curses
against the bare shop floor, working graveyard
to *get the bread together to sail around the world*—

It all changed meaning, then: *around the world*, *bread,* even
graveyard, eventually. First a metaphor for midnight, then
a place to spread a blanket on the grass. Finally, a barren field
sown only with regretful bones.

Even with another mouth hard against my own,
I felt you waiting: a man born sad, who then grew sadder,
a man left behind when he meant to be leaving,
still standing on the deck of neat boat manned
by tiny ghosts, a boat I think was named
for me: *The Sweet Kate,* I guess, or *Dance Calypso.*
Maybe *Summertime.*

August

We packed ripening fruit and crumbling biscuits to make a backyard picnic beneath hibiscus blossoms big as pleated paper plates, and jasmine, luscious and thick, spilling down onto our feast of color spread out on a patchwork blanket; crimson nectarines and peaches bleeding scarlet to a bright clear yellow, golden cherries and a single brown banana wanted only by the mayflies clouded by our ankles. Sparrows bickered above and a ripe fig fell to the yellowing grass, split and spreading sweetness, so much sweetness, sticky on our mouths and fingers. You turned to me.

Ghosts

This might be one of those movies where an angel shows you the life you could have
had if you'd chosen better, or worse, and then you wake up, or fall asleep, or open
your eyes, or jump off that bridge and find yourself, not struggling in a frigid river,
eyes and nose and mouth stinging with cold green water, flapping and flailing
despite your own resolute wish to sink, sink, be done with it—no, you're thrashing
in your own tumbled bed, and there's everyone all around you, the living and the dead,
your children, your mother, your grandfather with kindly eyes watching from the
corner and you're trying, really, to wake up, and the lover you do not have is patting
your shoulder and kissing your fragrant hair and whispering *it's okay, it's okay, oh,
you must have missed us, you must have been afraid.*

Rise

Sleep,
but set the alarm.
Dream,
but remember
the faint damp whisper
of your daughter breathing
in the dark, of your dog,
turning, turning, in his matted bed.
Remember the scent of milkflowers
tumbling over the front porch rail
and the bark of tires on the asphalt
beneath your bedroom window.
Remember that first cigarette, a cold
shower, the crisp folds
of your laundered shirt,
Remember the stink
of strong coffee,
brewed grudgingly by someone
who needs you still.

The Uses of Speech

(after Magritte, The Uses of Speech Triptych, 1928)

There we are still, somewhere, hand in hand
at the Brussels Museum, background in someone's vacation
shots: you, transfixed: *nuage, cheval, chaussee, fusil...*me,
baffled: *cloud, horse, road, gun...*catching on
to that earthbound *horizon*
like it was the last familiar thing I'd see, the last
of the old country, the one with both of us in it.

Me, hungry for color, texture, globs of paint piled up on canvas
like mushrooms wet and ripe against the forest floor. You,
satisfied with words, and dry ones.
Four masculine, one feminine, a pleasing ratio.
Charcoal on paper, shadow and light.

I'd gather those mushrooms, add wine and broth,
carrots—a chicken if I felt up to wringing its feathered neck—
and serve a stew of equal parts sustenance, hallucination, death.
We take our chances, don't we?
You'd crush them, kneeling to brush dust from a rock,
that we might sit awhile. That we might reconsider, soberly,
before moving on.
Cloud, horse, road, gun.
Horizon.

November

Tucking the receiver up under one ear, listening
for the baby with the other, mixing bowl pressed
against a belly softening with each November,
I listen without speaking: the rhythm of your outrage,
anger rising like dirty storm water, streaming
through that thumbhole in the dike. No child,
now, to stop it. Yours are grown and scattered
as we scattered once, thinking we'd return.

Does anyone? Now I've put the bowl aside as the baby
roots with a hungry mouth that someday will spit contempt,
then swallow it back, then press into a thin hard line:
the grim fix of my own mouth. How many years until
even this is sweet in memory? Your voice, cracks and static,
the baby's soft hand splayed against my throat, the smell
of death and sustenance rising from the oven like holiday song.

Kathleen

That thing you did
changed everything.
Oh, not for you. You're the same:
haunted, weeping—
tedious with it, actually.

But there's your niece—
the one you told, *It's okay
to be a little crazy*, except
now it's not.
That thing you did
changed everything.

Karen's baby turned sour
in her stomach. Kellen watches me
with narrowed eyes. *No one's next,*
I tell him. *Let's go on about our business
and get through this thing.*
The dog waits by the door
at five o'clock. I should have saved
her a shoe when the Goodwill
guy showed up.

Away

for Kathy

Crouching there, by the bald back tire,
you might be pulling roots from the black earth,
shooting craps, stirring the ashes of some archaic fire,
or tracing letters in the thickening soil, smelling leaves and bone
and loam rise against the swelling heat.
Your cheek is a wing, soft against the cool fender.
Last time: the shriek of crows, each blade of grass.

Now your fingers curl about a stiff cut hose, each separate
and determined to make this thing happen.

You released a falcon once, palms spread wide,
pushing him up, up into steep canyons of silvered clouds.

Your dogs will be snapping in the side yard, soon,
fearful and reluctant, but hunger-tamed
against the whispering uniforms, the jangled steel,
the deadening odor stirred by a thin breeze,
mingling with milkflowers, evanescent, and away.

It's All Shadows and Cats

Disconnect

So you're up at one to pay the electric.
If it went out, what would the neighbors say,
next door in their clean kitchen, gathered
at the breakfast bar like a family from a magazine –
but that's not what's wrong; that's not what you forgot.

That lump on the dog's side is tender
when you poke it with a careful fingertip. She licks
your hand, grateful for your eyes falling on her, your breath,
the smell of you. You rinse her dish, and fill it,
but that's not what's wrong; that's not what you forgot.

In bed again, curled in rough blankets damp with your own sweat
listening for the scratch of robbers at the door,
pigeons in the eaves, for your husband's soft grunt
as he turns, dreaming again, of what?
You, younger, maybe. Himself, before his face was like a mountain
carved from dirt: that cold, that secretly alive. You listen
for rats in the wall, for the paper at the door,
for your child's cry as she wakes, and slips beneath again;
there's food in the cupboard. There's gas in the tank.
You shut the iron off. That's not what's wrong.
That's not what you forgot.

Santa Monica Pier

At the end, there's no right or wrong to it,
just a stroll down the pier, the papers tucked beneath
your arm and my hand jammed in my pocket,
in case you might reach for it. If you felt the trembling
you would lead me to that cold water and let it
splash over us, wash over us, let the clean waves lift us,
huddled at the break. I can't do that again.
There's the chained lot where we smoked a joint
in your orange Bug, the one with the broken gas gauge
and a cracked sun roof: all the luxury we needed,
the moon watching over us like a kindhearted big sister.
And here's the booth where we took the photo our daughter
keeps taped to her vanity: that big eighties jumpsuit
I saved all month to buy, your hair slicked
off your forehead and both of us, young and dumb
as water in a cup.

Night is coming, for those with shelter
and for those without. Gulls are settling at the shore
where we lay past dusk, tracing letters in the sand,
and making plans, big ones. The sand is the same,
the water, the moon hanging shamefaced
over the blurred horizon, all our mistakes
piled up like driftwood behind us.

The Last Time I Saw You,

you were crushing a cigarette on the stone steps of the courthouse, scanning
the crowd but missing me, and I thought about a broad-shouldered boy,
awkward in a wide silk tie and borrowed shoes, and a girl in cream lace,
hair pushed back in a silky knot, both of them stuffing their pockets
with cash, mouths with powdered cookies, good wishes falling all around
like the first clean snowflakes in December, that dainty, that fresh,
that melting away forever.

and we moved together up the courthouse steps, dark words falling
all around like leaves in September, words like *ink spot,* and *leaving,*
and *mourning,* and *hunger,* words like *broken,* and *duststorm,* and
smoke-choked, and *gone.*

Esposito & Son

When the men arrived, finally, to haul the big table away,
I ran my hand down the battered length of it, as if along
the flank of some exhausted workhorse, overcome
by a sudden rush of absurd remorse. I'd never loved it,
being as it was first too shabby, then too grand,
for the way we lived (or should have lived, at least).

Six chairs, green velvet pressed flat, two more
with sculpted rests broad enough for a king's muscled
forearm (growing dusty in the basement, season upon season).
Two carved leaves should unexpected guests drop by, and these
still gleamed with polish though the tabletop itself was bleached
and scarred: ruthless curator of memory.

When the younger man went to fetch a blanket I bent
and laid my cheek flat against the cool mahogany.
The father shifted restlessly from foot to foot, eager
to be done with it, to be home, perhaps, king at his own table,
gesturing for his wife to slice the meat, to pass the buttered peas.

Three Things

There are three things worth noticing, he said, gulping latte from a doubled cup: *sunrise, sunset, and a pretty girl of any age; just those are enough to keep you going.* When you've been up too late, red wine rasping a hole in your gut, greasy chips around two a.m. and then that drunken call to the one you should have loved, but never could, despite this, you can leave the smoky confines of the small living room at the weak tail end of the night, sit out on the stoop where it's big, big, just air and space all around you, hardly a car or a barking dog, and breathe. There are the trees, as alive as you are: they're dinosaurs, that timeless, that vulnerable. Breathe in, breathe out, and let the horizon lighten and broaden with each breath till it's gold and orange and pink, morning breaking now; you've made it through. Later on, there's sunset. Same thing, but backwards, the wine still to come, the stumbling call, a cheap paperback until you're too bleary-eyed to see straight: dusk is a promise and it's one that gets kept. But the third thing, a pretty girl: maybe you are one, or used to be one, or once knew one. Maybe she's a tall slim thing with a short skirt and silly shoes, crossing State Street against the light, knob-kneed as a young giraffe. Maybe it's that neighbor upstairs who lets you use the phone when you get locked out, and she gives you sweet tea and pats the bar stool at her scratched kitchen counter. Maybe it's the infant you held for an hour at a party, all powder and milk, thick asleep in a waffled blanket—and the baby's mouth! A troubled wet rosebud, and her fingernails like pearlescent shells, each with its minute clean crescent at the tip. Oh, while we're living, let's drink in all this beauty! It made a certain sense, as things sometimes do, explained over coffee in a crowded shop, when you're not quite ready to face: well, the evening. The hollow room, the snapping clock, the stack of bills on the cracked piano. But when he got up to stretch I fingered his notebook, read the words scrawled in blue at the edge of the curling page: *Tonight I am so lonely, I might die.*

The National Geographic Society, 1968

Rainwater streaming, breaking and joining,
clear as brown agate, clear as marbles smacked hard
across another cracked walk, years ago, now.
Decades. Grass sprouting through the cracks, ragged
leaves of dandelion, cheap flowers cheerful
as a sun that was yellower then, and beneath the broken slabs
if you dared look, blind red worms, a potato bug
with fringed legs at the curve of its pearled shell,
fat cream-colored grubs, dappled slugs, beetles
with orange bellies, and always
that loop running, running in my head, like
nature films projected on a yellowed screen
in a darkened auditorium, tape crackling
and snapping: *an excellent source of protein,*
raw or pierced with a stick and broiled over flames—

(I would squat beside the men, their skins shining like leopard pelts. I would scorch the stick and
scarify my hard arms, I would wear my hair in matted knots with beads worked through, I would
be shirtless, flat and muscled like a man, like a cat. I would gorge on grubs like shish kebab, like
rinds of beef, like passion fruit, like honey—)

—Wednesday nights we'd board the groaning city bus
pushing past the weary workers coming home as we
were going out, three girls in prim dresses and white socks,
two boys chafing against starched collars.
At Society Headquarters we were all in a line like wild
ducks, like materyoshka, like Appalachian measuring cups,
filing neatly toward our usual row of grey metal folding chairs,

already lost in chimpanzee dreams,

grubs on sticks, smelted iron and gandydancers,

then a bus ride home in the deepening dark, drowsy now

between my brothers, just a girl again. Quarters tinkled

in a metal box beside the scowling driver whose bristled

neck rolled over his collar in grubby yellow folds.

The Five Children and It

The children stood round the hole in a ring, looking at the creature they had found… Its eyes were on long horns like a snail's eyes, and it could move them in and out like telescopes; it had ears like a bat's ears, and its tubby body was shaped like a spider's and covered with thick soft fur.

E. Nesbitt, The Five Children and It (1905)

We've stared too long into a cracked looking glass,
or rubbed a clean spit spot on the black brass lamp
or opened the wrong cupboard and tumbled
into this strange place, the five of us, our sister
bobbing grey pigtails and barking orders, our brothers
feckless and charming, bad knees and grizzled beards making
them at the same time the callow boys and the wise
professors of the stories we read so long ago, the ones
who knew the secrets of the cupboard, how to escape
the enchantment, how to live a whole life, then make it home
for tea before dark. And there's our littlest, solemn still,
pear-shaped and owlish, pointing out landmarks as we navigate
this cold land. We're in charge, finally—all our wishes granted:
What we like for supper, and cursing aloud, and some nights,
no bedtime at all; we sprawl about putting cigarettes out
in half-drunk foreign beers, like grown-ups. *Our father is dying,*
our sister shrieks. *But there are cards to play and debts to pay
and numbers don't add up right here.* Our shadows are shapeless.
I can't think what comes next. The little wants a story; that's my job,
even here, so I call them close and hand around sweets, wishing
the boys would do something clever with hairpins and sealing

wax, but they're slack-jawed, too, and waiting. I take her
little hand in mine.

> A long time ago, a long time ago, I huddled at the bus stop,
> a nickel clutched in one cold fist, but as each bus slowed
> I waved it away; it cost a dime to ride. The wind whipped
> my plaid skirt and chafed my cheeks and when the sun
> began to slide beneath the skyline, outlining the church
> in melting gold, I heard a faint cry, and turned, and
> there was our mother, arms open, coat
> flapping, and she
> was calling
> my name.

In Practical Terms

What it will mean then, is no one
left who remembers you before you
remember yourself. No one
to forgive the grey at your temples,
that roll of fat atop jeans that should
have been tossed a dozen years ago,
no one to overlook that bit of pettiness
at the florist last week, willing to forgive
just because they remember the weight
of you, the thick damp sweetness of you bundled
in your yellow blanket, a string of gold stars
on lined paper taped to the refrigerator,
the day you learned to read, to dance, to make spit
sisters, all arms and legs sunbrowned and
clean, pedaling away into a future that stretched ahead,
dark as an unlit road.

Because the Nurses Wore White

Those last days you found yourself on a vacation cruise
with relatives you'd shunned for years, glad
to know them, and to be known, baffled and pleased by
the rocking of the water, the neat portholes,
the smart cabin attendants—imagine, they'd come all the way
from Ethiopia, from Senegal, to make your ocean voyage!
The hospice guitarist played from the shifting deck, my
nieces brought desserts and tea, but you could not
be tempted, eyes fixed on that bright shore, glistening
with tears. It was hard to say what you were thinking,
your great jaw slack, big hands folded in your quiet lap.
My mother's cries might have been the tinkling of laughter
from the promenade, or the mewling of your firstborn sixty years
before, or they might have been the clink of cocktail
glasses, a murmur rising like smoke,
or they might have been a woman's cries, after all. Who
could have told me you were full of all the secrets
you're telling me now, as I sort your papers, listening
at last, knowing all the ways death changed you.

So This Is the Afterlife

You wait in your armchair or on the darkened stair
or in the glazed glare of pots that line
the patio, patient in a way you never were in life,
seeming to need only to know and to be known, folding
the newspaper, nodding until I draw too near. Then
it's all shadows and cats, as if I'd imagined you, imagined
the rustling, imagined this needling need to explain
the missed call, the forgotten card, the words that will
not be unspoken. It surprises us both, I think,
that I'm no longer young, and you—well. Better
not to say it. But I know you aren't there, and are
there. What we say or don't say can't change that.

I'm finding it easier to explain things
to you, than before you strode into that thick
blackness beyond the sky.

I remember standing hand in hand
on a hillside, searching for Andromeda;
You said I could be an astronaut, and I imagined
riding a bucking rocket to the stars, a space age cowgirl
in white boots and silver lamé, mesmerized
by the spark of tiny lights against the purple fabric
that cloaks the earth at night.

Sheba

All that beauty never got me much; strangers laying claim to what they think they recognize, every smile a promise, and most the kind you hope they won't keep. Beauty's an old dog that's too faithful, that sticks with you despite the curses and the kicks. They say it's a mask but it's the opposite in fact; it reveals what's inside, and everybody wants that sweet cream at the center of a chocolate éclair. What am I, now, but an old broad with glitter at her temples, scattered in her hair, yet I can't stretch on the bus without staking a claim. All that beauty never got me much but trouble, and a taste for trouble, a folded note, a couple of drinks at the bar.

When I Could Still Be Seen,

there was a party where I poured *grand cru*,
teasing other women's husbands till they were silly
with delight; there were turquoise boxes tied up
with pale ribbon, and a ramshackle hut on a cliff
at Big Sur, drenched in moonlight. A clumsy hand
traced silvered shadows along my naked hip,
before I vanished like fragrance, like fog.
There were armloads of scarlet roses,
and orchids like furled moths, a black spangled
dress, and glossy chocolates from Geary Street,
before I disappeared. A man draped a web
of coruscating stones against my throat
and lingered on the pulse, fingers thickened
with desire. This cloak of night,
this umbral shield, were not my first magic.
Once I held a boy to my breast as he raged,
and released him, gentled like a dog,
that grateful. I tapped nails like painted shells
against a compact of mother of pearl; I felt
the hot stroke of eyes against my taut skin.
When I could still be seen, I brushed by a man
in a blue cotton shirt and he sighed in wordless
longing and reached as if to catch me. I pretended
then to be invisible, as I truly am now, pushing
my hair into silken masses, then letting it go,
letting it go.

The Nature of Objects

There was a time traveler who moved
very slowly through time, and in just one direction,
in halting jerks, made baffled and headachy by dials
to pushbuttons, the dog's grey muzzle, a cracked lipstick,
her daughter's Easter shoes: first stuffed with paper,
then too tight, then tucked neatly in a carton
marked cheerlessly, *Goodwill.* Stumbling left,
then right, as if her limbs had grown too heavy,
or else too light, she ended staring at the window,
as the dirty river flowed, or flows, beneath the overpass
then swelled, overran, and dried again. Leaves flamed,
dried, dropped, the car died—the dog, too—while the daughter,
grown large as if by potion, telescoping distant
and close again, fled, came home, and finally shot
away, a comet trailing books, socks, blocks, outgrown skirts
and scratched CDs, a plastic cow, a spaceship.
And the traveler moved very slowly through time,
as if baffled by a bent enamel dish
that once held the dog's water, a cracked flowerpot,
by the layer of dust that conceals and reveals
the nature of objects, the crush of gravity, the thinness
of our atmosphere, the proximity of the sun.

DC, 1978

"The past is a foreign country—"
Leslie Poles Hartley

The past is another country; you can barely recall
your brief stay, stacking chipped red bricks
and boards for shelves in a room at the end of the hall

Painting sagging walls white in rooms so full of light
the rusted screens couldn't hold it all,
while down the block dogs barked warnings to the night

And there you are, leaning far out the window to call down
to a boy who smoked and loved to fight
and drive fast, a boy the girls said really got around

He never made it out. He lives only in that lost place
a cramped apartment in your hometown
And in his mother's candles, in her bewildered face

The past is a country of fruit-bright sky and bursting dawns
where you tip-toed home, carelessly laced
sandals slung over one finger, across dew-wet lawns

To find your sister awake, breathless, admiring and shy
your parents safe in their dull bed, radio on,
the front door bolted shut but every window flung wide—

ACKNOWLEDGMENTS

The author gratefully acknowledges the following first publishers. Some poems originally appeared in slightly different form.

Women Artists Datebook
  "Of Course, Some Are Very Small"
Yemassee
  "Tanager," "Jellyfish"
Tupelo Quarterly TQ9
  "Santa Monica Pier"
The Texas Poetry Calendar
  "Seven p.m."
Sequestrum
  "So This Is the Afterlife," "DC, 1978," "Gaia"
Poems and Plays
  "Onomatopoeia"
Nimrod International Journal
  "When I Could Still Be Seen," "The Five Children and It," "Feathers of Gold"
The New Yorker
  "Then Fall Again," "Sheba," "Esposito & Son"
The New Guard Literary Review
  "Because the Nurses Wore White"
Lunch Hour Stories
  "Or Maybe It's Für Elise…"
Iron Horse Literary Review
  "I See What We Must Become"
Fungi
  "The Uses of Speech"
Franklin-Cristoph Poetry
  "Heaven"
Flash Flash Click
  "While I'm Prostrate Before a God I Don't Believe in,"

Crab Creek Review
　　"Now That I Have Known Loss," "Save Me a Slice of Raisin Toast…," "Philadelphia"

The Comstock Review
　　"Twelve," "Around the World in Forty Years"

Compass Rose
　　"Grief," "Egg"

The Chickasaw Plum
　　"Kathleen"

Chautauqua
　　"Mississippi," "The National Geographic Society, 1968," "Wishbone," "Three Things,"
　　"Disconnect," "Babba Ya"

The Byron Herbert Reece Society
　　"Bacopa"

The Adirondack Review
　　"Away"

I am deeply grateful to Lisa Bickmore and to the board and staff of Lightscatter Press for taking me along on this inaugural voyage to the stars. Special thanks to Katharine Coles.

Deepest appreciation is due my mother, my daughter, and the memories of my father and sister, for unflagging support and enthusiasm.

Thanks to Susan G. for the nudge that changed everything, and to the memory of Kathy K., friend and muse, missed forever. Diana D., defining friendship. Thank you, Ellen B. and Frank G., for invaluable mentorship. Endless gratitude to Kevin, Hannah, Elisabeth, and Paul; I threw a bottle into the ocean...

Sincere gratitude to the editors of the publications, large and small, that first published many of these poems, and to the various judges who singled out my work for praise or encouragement.

Literary journals and small presses keep art alive. Support them!

Anna Scotti's poems have received a number of awards and honors. They can be found in The New Yorker and a variety of literary magazines. Scotti is the author of the young adult novel Big and Bad (2020), and her fiction appears widely. Bewildered by All This Broken Sky, her first collection of poems, spans more than 10 years' work.

When light encounters an object, it bends and scatters: as a form of energy, it passes through the air, then shifts and deflects in ways not entirely predictable. At Lightscatter Press, we seek to publish the work of writers whose writing diffracts as it meets the world, finding life and light in multiple mediums.

This book is set in Aaux Next and Minion Pro.
Book and cover design by Kayden B. Groves.
Printed on archival-quality paper.